CAN DO POWER

Embracing the Blessings
of Philippians 4:13

RAUSHANAH N. BUTLER

Order this book online at www.trafford.com
or email orders@trafford.com

Most Trafford titles are also available at major online book retailers.

Scripture quotations marked NIV are taken from the *Holy Bible, New
International Version®*. *NIV®*. Copyright © 1973, 1978, 1984 by International
Bible Society. Used by permission of <u>Zondervan</u>. All rights reserved. [<u>Biblica</u>]

Print information available on the last page.

ISBN: 978-1-4907-6889-2 (sc)
ISBN: 978-1-4907-6890-8 (hc)
ISBN: 978-1-4907-6891-5 (e)

Library of Congress Control Number: 2016900320

Trafford rev. 01/30/2016

 www.trafford.com

North America & international
toll-free: 1 888 232 4444 (USA & Canada)
fax: 812 355 4082

CONTENTS

This book is dedicated to two very important people in my life:
MY Superwoman, the Original Diva, my
Strength, my Mom - Pamela S. Prater
The one that encouraged me to be my best
self, my daughter - Joi K. Butler

You two have encouraged me in ways that are
unimaginable and for that, I am grateful.

INTRODUCTION

G od definitely has a sense of humor is all I can say. This book was birthed out of a sermon that I preached at a conference for battered women, women overcoming substance abuse and just women that were having a hard time period. The story behind this particular sermon was my own testimony and how just a short time before, I was a recipient of the conference due to major illness, major surgery, 2 sudden deaths, loss of employment, eviction and homelessness in less than 6 months. Yes, you read that right; but fast forwarding to the conference. For several days, weeks and even months after the conference, there were random women coming up to me and pumping their fists and yelling down grocery aisles, across parking lots and in the middle of restaurants "I CAN DO ALL THINGS THROUGH HIM WHO GIVES ME STRENGTH PERIOD!!!". It was surprising and humbling at the same time. What these women probably didn't know is that I was preaching to myself more than anything.

As time went on, life dealt blow after blow after blow, but God would always remind me of His Word and that sermon. More devastation met me in the form of more unemployment, bankruptcy, illness, a wedding being called off and then the ultimate for me: my Superwoman getting sick. Initially she was diagnosed with just having a stroke, but a year or so later it was determined that she has Multiple Sclerosis. I was crushed, I was shattered, I was numb, I was sad, and then I became angry and frustrated. The woman that I never saw sick (except for when she had to have gall bladder surgery), endured many hardships and heartaches, literally had a bounce in her step…was sick. She began making small improvements, and for a short time I was becoming excited about my Mom coming "home". Well, this happened in September of 2010 and she still hasn't "come home". She was in the hospital for a little over 2 years straight and eventually ended up in a nursing home. Her condition worsened and it resulted in an emergency double amputation above her knees with multiple hospital stays. But guess what? She's still here! Hospice has been called at least 3-4 times with one of those times being suggested for us to plan her funeral. But guess what? She's still here! She has endured several infections, fevers and viruses in the last several months. But guess what? She's still here! I don't know God's timetable for my Mom's life, but what I do know is that she is a fighter and is the epitome of someone that exhibits "Can Do Power". It is her fight that reminded me that this book still needed to be written as encouragement to walk boldly in the purpose that God has ordained for you. Why? Because you CAN!!!

CHAPTER 1

What Is Your Superpower?

"Don't be afraid of your own power." By Debby Ryan

Growing up I was always fascinated by superheroes. Whenever Wonder Woman, Superman and Batman came on, I was glued to the television. Although I knew in the back of mind that all of what I saw was fictional, there was something in me that always wondered what it would be like to be a superhero or to possess superhero powers. Come on! I can't be the only person that has ever wanted to be invisible, or was able to teleport myself from one place to another (even if it was just going from the bedroom to the bathroom), or even being able to fly. There was something about being able to do something someone else couldn't do that was attractive to me. Especially since these superheroes were also regular people. Even as a child, I never understood it, but now as an adult I've come to understand that each one of us possess a superpower of sorts. No matter how many people can sing, I'm quite sure that there will never be another Whitney Houston or Luciano Pavarotti. No matter how many people can paint, I'm sure there will never be another Pablo Picasso or Georgia O'Keefe. No matter how many people can entertain, I'm sure there will never be another Elvis Pressley or Michael Jackson. And for you, no matter what, there will never be another you. So what if there is another person that makes potato salad, if you know you make the best potato salad, own that. To put it plainly there will never be another person that cooks like you do, laughs like you do, dances like you do, motivate people like you do, or write like you do (yep, I'm preaching to myself).

All too often we get caught up in comparing our gifts with the gifts of another, failing to realize that because we are different it automatically makes our gifts different. God was so intentional about making each and every one us unique that no matter what we did, nobody could do it like us...whatever "it" is. So ponder this, what is your superpower? What are you created for, anointed for, appointed for, purposed for and gifted with to serve the world? What do you do so well, that you can do it with your eyes closed? 1 Corinthians 12:4-7 reminds us of this very thing:

> *There are different kinds of gifts, but the same Spirit distributes them. There are different kinds of serve, but the same Lord. There are different kinds of working, but in all of them and in everyone it is the same God at work. Now to each one the manifestation of the Spirit is given for the common good.*

One Sunday evening while eating gelato, my then 11-year-old daughter told me that she didn't think that people knew the difference between talents and gifts. She went on to say that talents are what you do, but gifts are what you are to do; that what God is calling you to do is in the spiritual and not the physical. I was blown away by her wisdom at such a young age, but even more blown away at the revelation. When we truly think about it, our gifts are given to us to serve the world not ourselves. 1 Peter 4:10 reminds us of this very thing: "Each of you should use whatever gifts you have received to serve others, as faithful stewards of God's grace in its various forms". So, once again, what is your superpower? And are you using it to serve the world? We all know that Jesus is the original superhero, but know that there is someone somewhere that has a need for what you have to offer.

POWER PRINCIPLE: You have a superpower, so use it!

POWER PLAY:

✝ Pay attention to the things that you do well naturally.

✝ Use a spiritual gifts assessment tool to discover what your spiritual gift(s) is/are.

✝ Evaluate your life and determine if you are currently serving in your gift area.

1) If not, what changes will you make and how will you make them?

2) If so, what can you do to continue to hone in your gifts?

✟ Once you've discovered your gift(s), it's time to move forward and put it/them to use; whether at home, in church, at work or in school. Use your gifts to serve them to the world.

POWER PLAYBOOK:

✟ Romans 12:3-8	✟ Proverbs 20:5
✟ 1 Peter 4:10-11	✟ Jeremiah 1:5
✟ 1 Corinthians 12:4-11	✟ 1Timothy 4:14
✟ Proverbs 18:16	✟ 2 Timothy 1:6-7

POWER PRAYER: *Most Wonderful and Wise God, I ask that You open my eyes, my ears and my heart so that it will be inexplicably known what I was created for, anointed for, appointed for, purposed for and gifted with. Your Word tells me in Psalm 139:13 that you created my inmost being and knitted me together in my mother's womb. You know everything about me and it is my prayer that I walk boldly in acceptance of what You created. Stir up the gifts within me Lord, that I may be used for the building up and edification of Your kingdom here* *on earth. I thank You for creating me to be a blessing to the world and I ask that you keep form any and every plot, plan, trick, trap, scheme or setup that they enemy has attempted to bring up against me to keep me from my purpose. It is so, in Jesus name...AMEN*

CHAPTER 2

I: It's All about You

"To be yourself in a world that is trying to make you something else is the greatest accomplishment". By Ralph Waldo Emerson

"There is no me, without you", "I need you to be complete", "Teamwork makes the dream work" and other clichéd quotes has been society's way of broadcasting togetherness and brotherhood/sisterhood. The desire to be needed, appreciated or accepted in some way, shape or form has formed gray areas in our lives when it comes to individuality, uniqueness and authenticity. It is an innate desire to be supported, encouraged and loved by others outside of self and immediate family. And don't be introverted...GEEZ! Truth is, when we accept who we are in God and start using the gifts He has given us, some of that "other" stuff won't even matter. Easier said than done right? Trust me, I get it. It wasn't until I was at a women's conference a few years back that it became a truth for me. Women were inspired, empowered and encouraged to embrace their gifts and talents and I was sitting there boo hoo crying like a baby. Not only was I in a funk, felt beat down and was totally discouraged; I suddenly felt like I didn't belong there. Here all of these beautiful women of different races, ages and backgrounds are pumping their imaginary fists in the air excited about the gifts they possess and ready to run with them. They held their heads high and had an air of confidence around them ready to take on the world. And silly me? I kept asking myself "Why am I here?"

It was hard for me to come to the full understanding that I too had something that the world needed (and wanted). More often than not, I was told that I wasn't good enough, smart enough, or pretty enough to amount to anything; and all of that kept replaying in my head at that very moment. Then this small woman came over to me and spoke something so incredibly powerful to me that it changed my life forever. Without missing a beat, she quietly said "You alone are enough because God is more than enough". It wasn't long before I went from crying over feeling sorry for myself, to lying snot-nosed on the floor and balling my eyes out over the fact that I doubted God. There's something I heard a long time ago that says that people don't have a Heaven or a Hell to put you in. And as it stood, I was in a private hell at the words of others, yet at the weaknesses of myself.

This is just a reminder that it is quite alright to be selfish at times when it comes to who are and Whose you are. I knew exactly what my gifts were and still felt beat down because I looked to others to validate me. If ever you felt like me, please understand that you are not a parking ticket; you don't need anyone to validate you. God put His stamp of approval on you the moment you came out of your mother's womb. You may have a quirky sense of style, a peculiar way of dancing, or always considered the "oddball" no matter who you're around... be you. Or you may snort when you laugh, have a silly sense of humor, or like sugar instead of salt in your grits...be you. You may even color outside the lines, have a unique way to decorate, or it might just be that you like to make loops at the end of your R's when writing your signature...be you. All in all, those things make you who you are. As frustrating and disheartening it may be at times, we must remember that it is the enemy's job to steal, kill and destroy; to steal your ambition, to kill your confidence and destroy your dreams so that you will forfeit everything that God has created you to do and be. In the end, don't spend your life being someone else so much that when the real you shows up, nobody recognizes him/her...not even you!

POWER PRINCIPLE: God made me fearfully and wonderfully, so it IS all good!

POWER PLAY:

- ✞ Who/What has you insecure?
    1) Is it a spouse constantly telling you that you're doing something wrong?

    2) A family member always bringing up your past?

  3) A boss/coworker attempting to make you feel incompetent at your job?

✞ How do you combat your insecurities? Is it healthy or toxic?

✞ When you look in the mirror, what do you see? List them here:

_____   _____

_____   _____

_____   _____

_____   _____

✞ When you look in the mirror, what do you WANT to see? List them here:

_____   _____

_____   _____

_____   _____

_____   _____

POWER PLAYBOOK:

✟ 1 Samuel 16:7   ✟ 1 Timothy 4:4

✟ Psalm 139:14-16   ✟ 2 Timothy 1:5-14

✟ Romans 12:2   ✟ Genesis 1:27

✟ Ephesians 2:10   ✟ 2 Corinthians 12:9-10

POWER PRAYER: *Hear the cries of your servant Lord that I may be heard. I've lived a life of hurt and shame due to me seeking validation and acceptance from others. I know your Word reminds me that I am fearfully and wonderfully made, so Lord help me to walk in that truth not just today, but every day. Put people in my life that are going to pray for me and with me, love on me, support me and encourage me when I find it hard to do those things for myself. Remind me that You are more than enough, and because of this, so am I. I thank You and praise You through it all. In Jesus name I pray...AMEN!*

CHAPTER 3

CAN: Ordinarily Extraordinary

"If you think you can, you can. And if you think you can't, you're right" attributed to Henry Ford and Mary Kay Ash

In most cases what we perceive our abilities to be is mind over matter; for we may need reminding that God created us to be *ordinarily extraordinary*. Dean Stanley sums it up by saying "The true call of a Christian is not to do extraordinary things, but to do ordinary things in an extraordinary way." There are several Biblical examples that can be used to demonstrate this concept. But there is a woman that I'm sure we can all identify with, the Samaritan Woman (or more closely identified as "The Woman at the Well"), that I believe can assist us in becoming "Ordinarily Extraordinary".

Let us take a glance at her story in John, Chapter 4. In verse 7, Jesus opens up the wave of communication by asking her to draw him a drink from the well. The Samaritan woman's rebuttal came quick, but filled with truth. Because in that time, Jews did not associate with

Samaritans in any way, shape or form. So her response was natural and more than likely a learned behavior. Let me stop right there. How many times do we respond to Jesus like this because of the behaviors we have learned in our childhood, though it has nothing to do with our salvation today? We're quick at professing the faith by which we have received Jesus as our personal Lord and Savior, but at the same time responding based on an engrained part of us that apparently has not disappeared yet. Spiritual growth will not happen overnight, but let us be mindful in how we respond to Jesus.

(Okay, now back to the Samaritan woman at the well with Jesus.) After the initial rebuttal, Jesus in turn gives her a glimpse into who he really is by offering her living water. The Samaritan woman missed what was being offered altogether because she answered in the natural. It is my belief that because of her sins, her mistakes and her problems; she was not open to receive what he was offering to her at that moment. Her vision was blurry and her ears were stopped up. Let us think on this a moment. Think back to the time before you found Christ and how your mindset was. You knew that there was more that you should be doing with your life and still steadily caught up in sin. Not necessarily because the sin felt good, but that's all you knew and was comfortable in that. It is human nature to reject anything that threatens our comfort zone. So as quoted by David Cottrell, "Our comfort zones can be our greatest enemy to our potential".

Jesus didn't let up though; in verse 13 he ensures the woman that if she takes what he has to offer, it can quench her spiritual, emotional, mental and physical thirst. And for the third time, she answered him in the natural. It can be argued that the woman knew who he was and decided to pick his brain to see how he would respond to her. It can be argued that the woman wanted to run him off my displaying ignorance. It can also be argued that the woman was ashamed and was trying to keep Jesus at bay. Whatever her reasons, in many ways she represents most of us before we came to Christ.

At this point, Jesus decided to turn the tables and prove that she has no choice but to believe. When her business was put out there and she then finally discovered that the Son of Man was in her presence, she dropped everything to go tell the people in the town. We can imagine the powerful testimony that she must have told; with much passion, much conviction and much humility because there stood the Son of Man who personally ministered to her.

Many of us tend to become fixated on our imperfections instead of allowing God to use us how we are. The next time we feel like God can't use us, just remember: Noah was a drunk, Abraham was too old, Isaac was a daydreamer, Jacob was a liar, Leah was told she was ugly, Joseph was abused, Gideon was afraid, Samson was a womanizer, Rahab was a prostitute, Jeremiah and Timothy were too young, David was an adulterer and a murderer, Elijah was suicidal, Isaiah preached naked, Jonah ran from God, Naomi was a widow, Job went bankrupt, John the Baptist looked like a wild man, Peter denied Christ, the Disciples fell asleep while praying, Martha worried about everything, Mary Magdalene was demon possessed, the Samaritan woman was divorced ... more than once, Zacchaeus was too small, Paul was a persecutor of Christians, Timothy had an ulcer...and Lazarus WAS dead!!!

POWER PRINCIPLE: God can use my ordinary self to do extraordinary things!

POWER PLAY:

✞ List at least 5 strengths you have:

    1.

    2.

    3.

    4.

    5.

✞ List at least 5 weaknesses that you have:

    1.

    2.

    3.

    4.

    5.

✟ What are some things from your past that you are still ashamed of?

_____

_____

_____

_____

_____

POWER PLAYBOOK:

✟ Romans 3:23

✟ Romans 10:9

✟ Romans 12:2

✟ Proverbs 3:5

✟ Story of Joseph – Genesis 37-47

POWER PRAYER: *Most Wonderful and Wise God, I thank You for showing me that just like the woman at the well, You can use me for a mighty work. Thank You for showing me* *that just like the powerful testimony that she went to tell the townspeople, You have also given me a testimony that I should not be ashamed of. I thank You for my strengths, but it is my weaknesses that You desire to use to bring people into Your kingdom. I release my past and my weaknesses to You right now in the name of Jesus, and ask that You remove any guilt from me that will hinder me for doing the work in which You have created me for. I love You Lord and I magnify Your name with the fruit of my lips. And it is in the precious name of Jesus I pray...AMEN.*

CHAPTER 4

DO: Fighting the Enemy of the 'Inner Me'

"Who needs enemies when you have yourself?
by Anonymous"

Let me share a personal testimony. Beautiful. Pretty. Cute. Gorgeous. Nice looking. Attractive. These were words that were never used to describe me. Instead, I heard words such as Tar Baby. Blowfish. Smokey. Lil Black Sambo. Gremlin. Ugly Duckling and so on and so forth. I was always told that my skin was too dark, I was too fat, my hair wasn't nice enough, I was too ugly and I was downright unattractive overall. The only time I heard that I was beautiful growing up was when it rolled off the lips of molesters. You don't see me in many pictures related to my past and every time I spoke to someone from my past, after the initial "How are you doing?" the question was either "What size are you now?" or "How are you wearing your hair these days?" It seemed as if my physical appearance was more important to them than my well-being. I thought that when I began dating, that I was found to be attractive. That quickly became only a fantasy when the general consensus was "You're fine, but you're ugly". Even not that long ago, guys that I've dated would never compliment me, but were quick to laud over women that they had no physical, mental or emotional tie to; instead everyone else in their eyes were beautiful, pretty, super cute, gorgeous or even sexy. I often cried myself to sleep at night wondering "WHAT ABOUT ME?!?!?!" I was never affirmed, poured into or validated as a little girl. So when I became a woman, everything shifted and I looked for love in all the wrong places because of it. This journey left me distanced from friends, drained mentally, emotionally conflicted and spiritually dead. I was incapable of loving anyone else, because truth be told, I hated myself. The day that it shifted for me was when I began to reflect on some of these negative words that I heard so often as I was journaling after my wedding was called off and eventually the relationship dissipated. I sat and cried softly and asked God why. A striking calm came over me and I distinctly heard God whisper in my ear, "My daughter you are created in my image, and those that know me see your beauty far beyond the artistic achievement I produced specifically before you were born in your mother's womb". WOW GOD!!! I believed the lie for so long that it ultimately became my reality, and the enemy that I was wrestling with was inside of me. I was so consumed with the constant negativity that was spoken over me and poured into me that I believed that is all that I was. Proverbs 23:7 reminds us that "for as he thinks in his heart, so is he" (NKJV). The sad part about it was that I wasn't the only person that thought this. Those that spoke over me believed the lie too because they didn't understand God's word that told me that I was fearfully and wonderfully made (Psalm 139:14). They didn't understand that when God created me, He said it was good (Genesis 1:26-31). They didn't understand that when God created me, He said that I was already formed in my mother's womb and that He knew me and sanctified me (Jeremiah 1:5). God took His time with me, down to the dimple on my right cheek. So many family, friends, loved ones and enemies cultivated that seed of low self-esteem that was planted so many years ago. I honestly thought that the skin I was in was a sin and that I was cursed to live a life of isolation because I wasn't attractive enough to be accepted on any level...friends, family or foe. NO LONGER!!! I am no longer bound by the insecurities of others and because I know God's Word, I know a lie when I hear one. And so it is for you as well, it really boils down to fully and wholeheartedly accepting God's love and in doing so, accepting that we are His masterpieces. No matter whether or not the world says no, if God says yes then you can DO it! I don't know what the "it" is, but we must first silence the enemy within before we can fully conquer the enemy on the outside. We can't do all that we were created to do if we only stand on the words of our naysayers. We can't do all that we desire to do if we consistently talk ourselves out of doing it because of what others might think. Let us not believe the lie of the enemy for so long that it is hard to accept that God has given us any of the gifts that we preach about to everyone else. Either way, it is my prayer that we silence the negative thoughts that have crept into our minds and take on the infamous slogan for Nike and "Just do it!"

POWER PRINCIPLE: I must do the thing I was told that I could not do!

POWER PLAY:

✝ What will you start trusting God to do in your life and what will YOU start doing as a result of that trust? List them here:

_____   _____

_____   _____

_____   _____

_____   _____

✝ When you look in the mirror, what do you want others to see? List them here:

_____   _____

_____   _____

_____   _____

_____   _____

POWER PLAYBOOK:

✝ John 1:12-14   ✝ Mark 9:24

✝ John 11:40   ✝ 1 John 4:1-2

✝ John 14:1   ✝ Colossians 3:17

✝ John 20:29   ✝ Romans 12:2

✝ Exodus 6:6   ✝ 2 Timothy 1:7

POWER PRAYER: *Oh Lord, my Lord, I am so grateful that You have opened up my ears to hear Your truth over the lies of the enemy. Please oh God don't forget about me, because there are times that I still struggle, so help me in my unbelief during those times that I may experience your grace and mercy seeing my shame undone. I declare your Words over my life and will walk boldly doing the things I did not think I could do. Renew my mind dear Lord, renew my heart dear Lord, and renew my spirit right now in Jesus name. To this I say YES LORD and thank You in advance for leading the way. In Jesus name I pray...AMEN!*

CHAPTER 5

ALL THIS: This AND That

"When I dare to be powerful, to use my strength in the service of my vision, then it becomes less and less important whether I am afraid" by Audre Lorde

The one positive thing that society has done a fair job of displaying is that people can do and be more than the labels that have been slapped on them since the beginning of time. There are television shows, movies, and real life examples that depict single fathers as successful businessmen; you also see children as successful students and business owners; there are women that balance being wife, mother and CEO; and you also have those single mothers that are in school, working and still maintaining their households. Is it easy? I'm sure it isn't. Is it worth it? I'm quite sure it is! You CAN have this and that, whatever your "this" and "that" consists of. There are four major components to having this and that and they are:

1) *Being sure of what it is that you desire to do and having the will to do it.* NOT what everyone else wants you to do, and how they want you to do it? Even the strongest of us have fallen prey to "people pleasing", but when you begin to focus on the purpose and not the people it will become much easier to put some elbow grease behind those dreams so that they become realities.

2) *Writing out your goals associated with your desire.* It is often said that if we fail to plan, then we plan to fail. Whatever God has impressed upon your heart to do and the gifts He has given you to do it/them are useless if you don't know how you are going to do it. You should be writing out your short-term (1 year or less), mid-term (1-5 years) and long-term (5 years or more) goals associated with this endeavor.

3) *Securing a support system.* NOT those that just give you support in speech, but in action. This is extremely important and not something that should be taken lightly. If you have kids and in school full-time, you will need to have a system in place for childcare if needed or to run errands concerning them when you cannot. Or even if you are completely single with no kids, having this support system will help you remain accountable to those gifts, talents, goals and dreams that God has given you to be steward over.

4) *Submitting the first three to God in prayer.* NOT telling God what you are going to do, but being sure that you are being guided by Him in all things. Because all too often we allow our emotional selves to take the lead in making decisions about our lives instead of our spiritual selves, and unfortunately we end up with permanent results based off of a temporary decision.

There is nothing proof positive when it comes to following your God-given dreams, but it is very possible to do all the things your heart desires, use the gifts you've been given and walk boldly in your purpose without having to make a decision on which one to pick or pursue. So, now that you know this, go ahead and do this AND that!

POWER PRINCIPLE: With God and a strong support system, I can and will do this AND that!

POWER PLAY:

✝ What are 3 endeavors I feel I'm being led to pursue?

1)

2)

3)

✦ It is never too late to get started, so what will it cost me to pursue these endeavors?(money, resources, time)

    1)

    2)

    3)

✦ What are your short-term, mid-term, and long-term goals associated with this desire?

_____   _____

_____   _____

_____   _____

_____   _____

POWER PLAYBOOK:

✦ Proverbs 21:5   ✦ 2 Chronicles 15:7

✦ Philippians 3:13-14   ✦ Habakkuk 2:2-3

✦ Philippians 4:12   ✦ Psalm 37:4

✝ Luke 14:28   ✝ Proverbs 29:18

✝ Hebrews 12:1-3   ✝ John 8:14

POWER PRAYER: *Father God, I am excited! I am excited because You have given me dreams, goals, gifts and talents to change the world. Lord, I submit them to you because I know that without your guidance, direction and covering, I will not be able to accomplish this and that. Open up my eyes, my ears and my heart to stay close to You so that every need is met and every desire comes into fruition. Use me to bless others with these endeavors and more importantly, for Your name to be glorified above all. In Jesus name I pray...AMEN!*

CHAPTER 6

THROUGH HIM: I Got the Power

"Power is not only what you have but what the enemy thinks you have. By Saul Alinksy, "Tactics," Rules for Radicals

It is always amazing that others think you have it all together when things in our lives have actually fallen apart. The beautiful thing about that is that though they may not be able to fully discern the source of this power we may seemingly possess, they know that we have the power. In the midst of that, heed this warning, the power attracts and repels based on the motive of the other person. That's where it become vitally important to maintain a prayer life synonymous with the life we live and the purpose we've been given. I used to always pray for God to give me the strength to match the territory that I asked Him to increase on my behalf. This wasn't a haphazard prayer, but one that was sincere because I knew that I would need the mental, emotional, physical and spiritual strength to handle the new and larger territories that I was beginning to walk into. And even with that, I knew that I wasn't walking alone. For in Deuteronomy 31:6 we are reminded to "be strong and courageous. Do not be afraid or terrified because of them, for the Lord your God goes with you; He will never leave you nor forsake you".

Now in this particular passage of scripture, the "them" refers to the Canaanites as Joshua and the Israelites get ready to cross over into the Promised Land after Moses successfully leads a mass exodus out of Egypt. But I'm asking you, who is your "them"? God has promised you that you will possess the land (whether that is in the form of starting a new business, restoring your marriage, going into ministry, finishing school or writing a book) and you are on the edge of that land, but for some reason you've forgotten that you have the power. So He reminds you yet again that He will never leave you nor forsake you. You have already established what was holding you back, and began to move forward. You have identified your strengths and weaknesses associated with your past and present, and you've even written your goals down. You are ready to take that leap of faith, but a tinge of fear stops you from jumping all the way in and you remain content with just putting your feet in the water to test the temperature. No ma'am and no sir; that is not the way to go. Let me give you an example. I and my daughter both have cell phones that require the same charger and we go through phone chargers maybe twice a year. But one time in particular, I had just bought a charger and it wasn't working properly. Of course, I was frustrated and even vocalized that because I just purchased it. After turning my phone off and on, taking the back off and reinserting the battery, and everything else I could think of; it was discovered that though the charger was plugged all the way in, the port wasn't completely plugged into my phone. Get it? The source was fine and ready to go, but my phone wasn't completely plugged into the source! That may be where you are and the reason you can't fully step over into your Promised Land, but don't allow it to be 40 years (like the children of Israel did) before doing so. Have faith in The One that has created you, anointed you, appointed you and ordained you for such a time as this. It is time for you to tap into the power source so that you can fully possess the land promised, and in return for others to be recipients of your divine purpose.

POWER PRINCIPLE: I got the power, not it's time for me to use it!

POWER PLAY:

✝ What has been your "them" that has kept you from crossing over into your Promised Land?

_____

_____

_____

_____

✝ What are some things that are keeping you from fully tapping into the "power source"? List them here:

_____   _____

_____   _____

_____   _____

_____   _____

POWER PLAYBOOK:

✝ Exodus 14:14   ✝ Matthew 7:7-8

✝ Proverbs 3:5-6   ✝ Matthew 17:20

✝ Psalm 1:1   ✝ 2 Corinthians 8:11-12

✝ Psalm 46:10   ✝ Jeremiah 29:11

✝ Hebrews 10:35

✝ John 14:26

POWER PRAYER: *Most Wonderful and Wise God, I come to You ashamed that I have sat on the edge of my blessing and let fear stricken me. You have been with me every step of the way and I've allowed people, things and situations hinder me from fully tapping in You and taking possession of my Promised Land. Today I shall walk boldly in faith knowing that You will still be with me, as I pray to You, read Your Word daily and cultivate my relationship with You. In Jesus name I pray...AMEN!*

CHAPTER 7

WHO GIVES ME: It's Still Personal?

"We have to dare to be ourselves, however frightening or strange that self may prove to be". By May Sarton

Even with establishing a support system, having accountability partners, or sharing with our spouses, family, friends and loved ones…it is STILL personal. Because the truth is, none of them will be able to successfully live out the purpose that God has for you. Maybe God has given you the greenlight to write your life story (speaking to myself), and despite whether there are those that are ready to purchase the book, you have outlets in place to market the book, and even workshops planned out associated with the book, NONE of that will happen until YOU write the book. Or maybe God has impressed upon your heart to start a food and clothing pantry for the less fortunate families in your immediate community. And instead of looking at the needs that will be met, you're stuck on those that laughed at your idea (remember, we can't share our dreams with everybody), frustrated at the lack of finances you think you need to pull it off and starting to question if this is what God really wanted you to do. Whatever that hindrance is, it still won't be done unless you do it

It matters not what others are doing or aren't doing, it matters not who is supporting you and who isn't, and it matters not how long it will take to get it done. What matters is again, you are the person that is supposed to be doing it. If Steve Jobs would have waited on approval from everything and everybody, we wouldn't have one of the greatest technology companies in which to choose some of the most innovative computers, phones and now watches from. If Oprah Winfrey stayed stuck on the abuse she endured as a child, and the fact that she was told that she wasn't fit for television, she would not have pushed to become one of the most recognized names and faces of all time. If Thomas Edison allowed the words of his teachers to penetrate his heart and keep him from pursuing education, he would not have been integral in the invention of the light bulb. Martin Luther King Jr. was said to be initially shunned by his family because he chose a different career path. It is still mind boggling to me that Walt Disney was fired from a newspaper job because they said that he didn't have any good ideas and lacked imagination. And let's not forget the Virgin Mary. What an assignment she had. Just think, God could have chosen a different woman, a different method and a different time for Jesus to be born. Instead He specifically chose a young virgin girl to carry out a sacred task. WOW! What does that say to you? Regardless of whether the world has said no, all you need is one yes from God; and God gave you the greenlight when He created you...yes, YOU! The world is waiting on what you have to offer, so dare to be your authentic self and change the world one book, one play, one business, one song, one idea and simply one step at a time!

POWER PRINCIPLE: It's not all about me, but it's still about me, so I must accept my assignment and do great works for God's Kingdom.

POWER PLAY:

✞   It may not be a business idea, or even a ministry, but what's something that God has been tugging at your heart to do? And why haven't you done it?

_____

_____

_____

_____

_____

✞   What are some things about you that are unique that you need to start celebrating? List them here:

_____   _____

_____   _____

_____   _____

_____   _____

POWER PLAYBOOK:

✝ John 8:32   ✝ 1 Peter 2:9

✝ John 4:24   ✝ Ephesians 2:10

✝ John 17:17   ✝ Romans 11:36

✝ James 2:18-26   ✝ Psalm 138:8

POWER PRAYER: *My Creator, I am in awe of Your work. Before my days came into being, You knew me and purposed me. Lord, I thank You for every imperfection, every flaw, every quirk and every unique feature that You have given me because it reminds me that there none other. You created me with a specific purpose in mind and I trust that purpose with You as I move forward in it. I thank You simply because of who You are and I will glorify You in all that I do. In Jesus name I pray... AMEN!*

CHAPTER 8

STRENGTH: I Can't Be a Superhero…All the Time

"When we long for life without difficulties, remind us that oaks grow strong in contrary winds and diamonds are made under pressure". By Peter Marshall

The one main misconception about the superhero complex is that most people believe that this person is strong all the time. It's quite the opposite. Going back to what I mentioned in Chapter 1 about some of my favorite superheroes is the fact that they were still very regular people. Superman was also Clark Kent, Superwoman was also Lois Lane and Batman was also Bruce Wayne. Their human selves revealed their idiosyncrasies, their true personalities and ultimately their weaknesses. They couldn't be superheroes all the time. Truthfully, if they were it wouldn't serve their purpose well because their superhero personas thrived off of the fact that there was another side to them. If they were always superheroes, when would they rest?

When would they enjoy the others elements of life that it has to offer? How would they be able to cultivate their other gifts and talents? Who would they be able to truly associate with, fellowship with, be in relationship with and in community with? What legacy would they leave outside of the one tied to their "mask"?

Yes, we are to walk in our purpose, but we can't walk in it and fulfill it successfully if we are worn out, burned out, broken down, busted and disgusted. Sometimes we have to set aside the cape that we wear most times and obliterate the picture of perfection (because if we were perfect, there would be no need for Jesus). Sometimes people need to see our tears, hear our frustrations and witness our mistakes. It is okay to be vulnerable. Not to the point of being taken advantage of, but to the point that we are real. One of the worst things we could ever do is to put on a façade as if we have it all together, and then everything falls apart. That does a disservice to the people that are assigned to us and our assignment overall. So never be afraid or embarrassed to struggle, because there is no shame in doing what needs to be done to ensure success.

I will never forget when this became true to me. It was a typical day for me. Work, networking event after work, my daughter's basketball game and then a meeting at church. It wasn't until the end of the meeting when we were gathered for prayer that it happened. BAM! I hit the floor. Hard. When I finally came to, I had a massive headache and was a little disoriented, but for the most part I was fine. I went to work the next day (yes, I know I was hardheaded), but my headache was so bad that I ended up in the emergency room only for them to keep me. After running a battery of tests, me missing my daughter's band concert (which increased my blood pressure), and vials of blood being taken seems like from everywhere, it was determined that the cause of my fainting spell was exhaustion and stress. See, I was so busy being superwoman that I never took the cape off. We have to be certain that in the midst of these tasks assigned to us that we don't overexert ourselves. Our minds may think we are handling everything well, but our bodies stop when they have had too much. So yes, it is okay to take your cape off every now and then so that you can be mentally, emotionally, physically and spiritually healthy.

POWER PRINCIPLE: When I'm weak, then I am made strong!

POWER PLAY:

✞ It is vital that we rest so that we can be replenish everything we pour out, what are some things you do for "me time"? List them here:

_____   _____

_____   _____

_____   _____

_____   _____

✝ Even while you are resting, where is your cape stored? Is it easily accessible? Or are you truly allowing yourself to rest?

_____

_____

_____

_____

_____

POWER PLAYBOOK:

✝ Isaiah 41:10	✝ Jude 1:24
✝ 1 Corinthians 2:3	✝ Matthew 11:29
✝ 2 Corinthians 12:9-10	✝ 1 John 1:9
✝ Ephesians 6:10	✝ Romans 12:1
✝ Hebrews 4:16	✝ 1 Peter 5:7

POWER PRAYER: *Lord, I get tired more than a little bit, but I'm grateful that You reminded me that I need to rest. Help me* *to put into practice those things I encourage others to do so that I can healthy in all facets of life that You have given me. I pray for good health, being in my right mind and have the physical capacity to achieve the things You set before me. As part of my charge I will make sure I seek medical attention when needed, keep regular checkups, eat right, exercise and simply rest when it is needed. I love You Lord and I will take care of the body You have given me. In Jesus name I pray...AMEN!*

CHAPTER 9

PERIOD: It Is Finished

"I decided I can't pay a person to rewind time, so I may as well get over it". By Serena Williams

You may be excited and ready to move forward in whatever God has for you, and may have actually completed a task; but there's a small voice in the back of your mind asking several "what if?" questions. What if it doesn't work? What if it's bad timing? What if I don't get the support I need? What if I life changing event occurs in the midst of everything? What if my restaurant fails? What if people don't buy my book? What if my mentoring program doesn't get any applicants? What if my grades drop in school? What if? What if? What if?!?!?!? Well, the thing about that is that even if those things were to happen, the past is as early as yesterday and you have today to try it all over again. That's a blessing in and of itself. To know that we are presented with a new day to try something new, attempt something different or start over altogether.

We embrace the time we wake up as the beginning of a new day. We embrace the first of the month as the beginning of a new month. We celebrate our birthdays as the beginning of a new season. And we set goals and make resolutions on New Year's Eve as the beginning of a new year. Let us do the same thing as it relates to any mistakes or mishaps that we may make. The old saying goes, "Why cry over spilled milk?" reminds us to not be upset or sad over something that can't be undone. Simply put, get over it! I know, I know, that may sound a bit harsh, and it is not an intent to be insensitive. So cry if you have to, scream if you must, but after that is over it is time to pull your big girl panties and big boy drawers up and start anew.

When you look at the scripture for which this book is based upon, Philippians 4:13, it reads "I can do all things through Him who gives me strength." There isn't a comma, there isn't a semi-colon, but there is a period. A period at the end of a sentence is recognized as a full stop. With the next idea, thought, concept or issue starting in a new sentence. So that being said, as it is written, you can do all things through Him who gives you strength PERIOD! God said it, now believe it, and that should settle it!

POWER PRINCIPLE: I can do all things through Him that gives me strength PERIOD!

POWER PLAY:

✝ Be honest with yourself. What are the "what if" questions you're wrestling with?

_____

_____

_____

_____

_____

✝ Because you now know the truth about your "what if" questions, replace each question with an affirmation associated with it.

_____

_____

_____

_____

_____

POWER PLAYBOOK:

✝ Philippians 4:13	✝ Ecclesiastes 12:13
✝ 1 Corinthians 12:11	✝ James 1:4
✝ 1 Corinthians 15:57	✝ Romans 4:21
✝ 2 Corinthians 9:8	✝ Proverbs 16:8
✝ Ecclesiastes 3:1-8	✝ Matthew 6:33

POWER PRAYER: *Lord, You said it, so I'm going to trust You at Your Word. Because I am human, I'm prone to mess-ups and mistakes, but I know that Your grace and mercy abounds. Even in my ignorance, give me a thirst for knowledge and unshakable desire to seek Your wisdom. And even if I do fall prey to my own condemnation, help me to forgive myself, get up and look up so that I may move forward. I thank You for being my Sun by day and my Moon by night, guiding me at all times. And it is my sincere prayer that people come to You due to the works You have blessed my hands with. In Jesus name I pray…AMEN!*

POWER PONDERING – *You Now Have the Power… USE IT!*

> *"Mastering others is strength. Mastering yourself is true power". By Tao Te Ching*

We can spend a lifetime learning, but if we don't apply what we have learned, then most times it is all for naught. One doesn't learn to cook only to never cook again, or learn how to ride a bike just because, or write books just to say that they've written a book. There is always a desire attached to a purpose, and once we combine the two, we share it with others. Yes, our purpose is ours, but in the grand scheme of things, it is about everyone but us. It's always a beautiful experience to watch other share what they know with others. You can see the energy, hear the passion and feel the anointing when someone is walking in their true, authentic purpose. Just remember at the end of the day, we are answering to God and will have to give an account of the gifts, talents, dreams and resources He has given us to be stewards over. Knowing what you know, the account should be thoroughly positive because you can do all things through Him who gives you strength!!!

I can do all this through Him who gives me strength.

I CAN do all this through Him who gives me strength.

I can DO all things through Him who gives me strength.

I can do ALL THIS through Him who gives me strength.

I can do all this THROUGH HIM who gives me strength.

I can do all this through Him WHO GIVES ME strength.

45

I can do all this through Him who gives me STRENGTH.

I can do all this through Him who gives me strength... PERIOD!!!